LET'S EXPLORE SOUTHEAST ASIA
(MOST FAMOUS ATTRACTIONS IN SOUTHEAST ASIA)

BABY PROFESSOR
EDUCATION KIDS

Southeast Asia is located in the southeast portion of the continent of Asia. There are around 20,000 islands in Southeast Asia.

Angkor Wat is a temple complex in Cambodia and the largest religious monument in the world. Angkor Wat has become a major tourist destination. Angkor Wat is the primary reason that more than 50% of international tourists visit Cambodia.

The Grand Palace is a complex of buildings at the heart of Bangkok, Thailand. The Grand Palace is currently partially open to the public as a museum, but it remains a working palace, with several royal offices still situated inside.

Mount Kinabalu is the highest mountain on the island of Borneo in the east Malaysian state of Sabah. It is one of the world's most important biological sites.

The Petronas Towers are twin skyscrapers in Kuala Lumpur, Malaysia. Petronas Towers are the tallest twin buildings in the world. There are 88 stories in Petronas Twin Towers.

Coron Island is located at the northern tip of Palawan in the Philippines. Snorkeling and diving are two of the most famous and sought-after activities.

Wat Arun is a
Buddhist temple in
Bangkok, Thailand.
The temple's
full name is Wat
Arunratchawararam.
Named after the
Indian god of dawn
Aruna, Wat Arun
is best viewed
during sun set.

Borobudur is a 9th-century Mahayana Buddhist Temple in Magelang region of Central Java in Indonesia. Borobudur is Indonesia's single most visited tourist attraction.